The Secret Diaries of Jean Batiste

The Secret Diaries of Jean Batiste

Nigel Walker

The Secret Diaries of Jean Batiste

ISBN: 0-9754357-0-1 (paperback)

Cover design by Anwar Thomas

For information:
Kobalt Books L.L.C.
P.O. Box 771912,
Saint Louis, MO 63177
Printed in the U.S.A
www.kobaltbooks.com

To
My mother, Jacqueline
My sisters Cecilia, Aisha, Earlona, Roberta, and Robin
My brothers Anwar and Jared
The rest of my family
My friends who have been with me all the way
And the ladies who allowed me to use them as
inspiration.

Thank You.

Nigel

Introduction

An undiscovered treasure has risen amidst the ashes of burned time. The diaries of a starving poet were found and their contents revealed. Inside the fragile pages lie the words of what seemed a hopeless romantic. The whereabouts of the author and the subjects acknowledged in his verses are unknown. How long the diaries have been lost is also unknown. All is known is what he describes of himself in his two autobiographical pieces found in the beginning. The writer also makes known the great passion for those discussed as each poem written is dedicated to whom may have been his love at a particular time. Though the names were left out, it would be no trouble for the subjects to recognize which work is to them. However, he meant for his feelings not to be publicized. Such can be seen through the title sketched at the beginning of his great work at the time of discovery— *The Secret Diaries of Jean Batiste.*

The Secret Diaries of Jean Batiste

Jean Batiste

Mine is a lineage of great descent

Extracted from the veins of the ancient French.

But if my tone dreads such a line

It's from the concoction of blood in time.

For the race from which I drew my shell

Has but a more solemn ancestry to tell.

The Batistes from which I am drawn

Were bound by the fruit of their labor--dusk till dawn.

I swear by the name in pride

Though their lives were driven as a mule's ride.

So I am Jean Batiste of French decent

of luck's merciless neglect to leave me bent

as the leaf of life manipulated by the wind,

till its blown from this place at life's end.

I am Jean Batiste of the Batiste line

whose trials in time show in the struggles of mine.

9

The Secret Diaries of Jean Batiste

Yet inevitable paths shake me in the least;

for I am the strong, proud Jean Batiste.

Mr. French (Jean Batiste - part II)

You know me, I go by Jean Batiste and they don't call me Mr.

French for nothing.

I look around and see a lot of frustration on the ladies faces

As if they were missing something.

That is where I step in—or should I say creep—to leave you

crawling on the inside

From a feeling so deep in the sea of satisfaction that

emotional control cannot survive.

I don't claim to be your superman, but I contain remedy

To the pleasure, impostered by the last man, who only

reflected inferior intimacy.

The Secret Diaries of Jean Batiste

One jewel in which I hold my strength is locked within these

two hands,

For what love needs is a pillar of patience on which to stand.

My hands will take the time to journey your temple in its

entirety,

With a touch so pure caressing each limb that it resounds an

essence of virginity.

Then I start to brush my lips across the nook of your ear

And kiss the nape of your neck, forcing it into motion;

saturating you in salivation;

Lubrication with oral lotion.

I then follow the path of your frontal valley, from your chest

to naval

And trace my journey back several times,

I suckle your breasts as if within them lies nectar of my

goddess's vines.

The Secret Diaries of Jean Batiste

I return my southward advances to the fertile banks of your

feminine loins

And partake in the consumption of my surroundings

fiendishly over your form.

Rapid impressions congest your canal inciting episodic

outbursts.

As inklings of your pleasure softly sing out, enticed by

centripetal forces.

Then gravity pulls me deeper to the core where which your

love erupts.

You arise relieved that you survived such an act of nature,

But realizes that this was only foreplay...

Dedications

A Song For Kiara

You came to me like a dream

And so it seemed that this was all unreal—the things that I

feel.

But when you kissed me I knew that it was true

Even though in my mind, it was impossible to find

Such a beautiful angel. We were like perfect strangers.

You must have come down from heaven

Because only God can be responsible

And it's so good to be here with you.

I just want to behold you Forever.

Lady, before you came

Cloudy days brought sadness in my windowpane;

My sorrows so deeply stained.

13

The Secret Diaries of Jean Batiste

Then a ray of your love shined on me

And filled my heart with clear skies

With the sparkle of your bright eyes.

I can't possibly see

how heaven could surrender such a treasure to me.

Now that I have you I don't want to lose you.

You are so special in my heart. I knew from the start

That heaven must have sent you.

And now that you're here with me

I hope that someday this will be

An eternal love

Since you traveled from so far above.

And all of the love we'll share

Can nothing in this world compare

To what we have

It is truly heavenly.

The Secret Diaries of Jean Batiste

If heaven only knew what it's given me,

Would I be worthy of you being mine?

If heaven only knew what it's given me,

God would probably spare you for the next lifetime.

Black Queen

Ebony rivers of her silky, rich hair washes away all conjured

thought;

That to utter a single spoken word is miraculous in her

presence.

Her caramel skin salivates my temptations as I lose control of

all my senses.

Just to see her, feel her, taste her affections would soothe the

yearning built by capturing her essence.

Her voice commands my emotions; that I fall to her feet,

surrendering to her will.

Looking into her eyes throws me into a trance; I am trapped

in her luscious aura.

She has enslaved my soul into her ownership; she is the ruler

of my burning desires.

The Secret Diaries of Jean Batiste

She is a queen--not of a material throne, but of the love that

pulsates in my veins, stemmed from my heart that bleeds

attraction to her celestial beauty as a yonder star.

A beauty extraordinarily causing my grief; for I came skin-

close to my heavenly mirage, but in an instant my treasure

ceased to be.

Disguised as a gentle kiss, only soft winds passed ;

disappointment then drew a single teardrop, but perseverance

began to build within.

I shall vow to reclaim her heart whether she is living or

legend; in that I know inside her exists a mortal being

susceptible to my subtle hints passed when our eyes meet.

Though we come from diverse worlds, we share a common

orbit.

To be one world, one mind, one heart is a yet un-reached

goal, but to be continued...

The Secret Diaries of Jean Batiste

Beautiful Blossom of Nature's Bosom

Beautiful blossom of nature's bosom

Struck from earth with rich complexion,

Ebony goddess and temptress

Suffer me a taste of your perfection

For long I have sought your glorious shores;

The fertile loins of your smile;

The natural curves cut in your body.

Let me hold you like luck being destiny's child.

Slowly we will take our course

To enter a realm of tender love

As pure and deep as our souls can,

Releasing our emotions gracefully as a dove.

Conversation running as smooth as your skin

The Secret Diaries of Jean Batiste

Taunting the feeling of you and I

Speaking softly, I petition your mind,

"Let's get lost in each other as time goes by."

Such a delicate gem of beauty

Needs the softest heart on which to lean

"So, here. I hold out my hands to you

To take you as my queen."

And indeed I will squeeze you tightly

As not to lose you to a material world

Yet gently you will find my hands likewise

Caressing my invaluable pearl.

The Secret Diaries of Jean Batiste

Relations

Reading my advances,

We exchange deep glances;

As the tempo slows,

Our mental captivity glows.

Waltzing to the song of love,

Our hearts become as tender as a dove.

We are filled with innocence like unto a first chance;

Our souls unify as we dance.

Hand of interlocking joy

Lead our bodies' journey. We begin to deploy,

Deep into the thought of affectionate rapture;

I feel the very sensation I longed to capture.

Holding on from the intensity of our motion,

The aroma fills the room of lover's potion.

As roses dipped in the essence of sweet nectar.

Our bodies lie as a passionate specter.

The Secret Diaries of Jean Batiste

S.O.S. (Someone Special)

Everything about her sparks my interest.

She draws me to conversation as if being a temptress.

Her personality soothes my ambitions.

As I journey to acquire her attention on an impossible

mission.

She has an inner peace that glows about;

Contagious in the joy it spills as it spews out.

Capturing all souls, lost in the world,

Her qualities exist as scarce as discovering a pearl.

But I have found my priceless jewel

In the reminiscent moments, which pumps the fuel

Igniting a passion to be in her presence,

Knowing that her temple is royalty—I, merely a peasant.

Hoping to only touch the hem of her appeal,

Anticipation leaves me congested with the feelings I feel.

Lifetimes to come, we are apt to combine,

So I hope to share a common light in which to infinitely

shine.

Tipsy

Intoxication puts me in boxed matrices—incarcerated

Bound by passion crimes committed in my mind;

Taking crystal shots in consumption of attraction strong as

brandy,

Straight knocking a brother off-balance.

The challenge is to give it a smooth taste

As I ingest it, and invest a dyme to my mental savings.

Yeah it's like that so I won't lie,

My glassy eyes show my daze when I stumble over mental

blocks

Put in cognition's way with each new sip of thought.

The hour glass tips and spills the contents,

A sandy, smooth substance resembling what's in my system.

I'm under the influence;

The Secret Diaries of Jean Batiste

Swerving, slurred speech, staggering, and just a little tipsy.

In love with the distorted realities;

Over the limit of my B.A.C—my bodily attraction is content

with what I see before me;

Relying all judgment on my goggle vision.

Yet and still I live by my condition; being drunk off of that

love potion.

The Secret Diaries of Jean Batiste

Unseen Truth

She sees right threw me as if she never knew me

But how often were her eyes actually drawn to me?

She grips her heart so tightly that it suffocates, suffers to

communicate, and complicates connection to me.

And how often has my touch shaken her composure, and

dulled her senses that in sudden instances, love songs sang in

thoughts of me?

How can it be that she denies my hand?

Maybe she can't comprehend the actions of a real man.

One who has already measured a woman's worth,

Show the most precious jewels or greatest weight in pure gold

is only a fraction of the priceless moments I deem worthy of

her presence.

Yet her closed mind makes the figures obsolete.

Even though her meter runs when our eyes meet and

compete with her racing heart,

The Secret Diaries of Jean Batiste

She still forfeits her feelings to the notion that we are

opposites—not fit,

Which puzzles me.

And if I agree to let go, she glares in opposition, but her

physical position remains to the naked eye

Undressing the truth that something lies beneath to one day

surface and expose that she has love for me.

The Secret Diaries of Jean Batiste

Your Servant

How would like your passion served?

With shrimp and wine or just tender verbs?

I carry you to ecstasy's inn, well lit with candles.

Now lets begin.

I lay you down on the flowered sheets, laced with rose petals

a half –inch deep.

I bathe you gently from head to toe that the extent of your

body has the hint of rose.

Stroking your temple, soft and sweet, I tickle your emotions

with my voice's beat.

My words finessing your soul, you quietly moan as you lose

control.

Our engagement still in an early stage, temptations arise in a

lustful rage.

The Secret Diaries of Jean Batiste

Not to rush our gentle flow, I massage your tension; you let it
go.

The mood now very smooth and mellow, we dance to the
night creatures' bellows.

Their songs of romance sensuating the night, we continue our
escapade well into the twilight.

I work my way around your every curve; you tremble as
though I struck a nerve.

Your vibes expressing your very thoughts, yet temptations I
continually fought.

For love takes time even in heated passion, so I take a deep
breath in a calming fashion,

Then proceed to caress your thoughts occurring; by now the
butterflies are frantically stirring.

The Secret Diaries of Jean Batiste

Our pounding hearts strike in our ears as though we suffer
incredible fears,

But this anxiety appeals in such times as we celebrate our
synchronized minds.

Both knowing what deeds are in store, we embrace the
feelings that start to pour.

Sweat beads about your neck, glistening on your body like
diamond specks.

I obtain the riches awaiting acquisition; your body flexing to a
just position.

As if drowning the moment, you hold your breath—it seems,
a minute.

You then exhale, gazing with glassy eyes and song sang out
like unto an angel's cries.

The tempo slows to a steady pace and satisfaction runs down
your face.

The Secret Diaries of Jean Batiste

I dreamed, your servant I would work in haste.

My duty filled, I wallow in your grace.

The Season

Silhouettes dancing in the flickering candlelight;

Dim lights are mellowed with the sweet smell of winter mints;

Fresh, crisps currents of the artic breeze chill my mind to

perfect serenity.

The spirit of the season sparkles in the smile of each bright

face passing by.

Yet, I only gaze across at an angel whom I am cuddled closely

for her warmth.

My sub-conscience pulls me into a solemn fantasy.

As all unconceivable moments of happiness blossom, I grasp

them with my heart

And close my eyes to absorb them eternally;

Vividly imagining gazing up at the luminous twilight skies

That encircles a heavenly crown around my true love's

beauty;

Breathing her as a sweet rose's scent,

The Secret Diaries of Jean Batiste

Unmoved by the thorns that prick in my every day's situation.

For at the top I reach the delicate petals of her body,

Soft as a feather bed in the sky,

Unable to hold the heavy weight of imperfection.

All that exists are our free spirits entangled in the clouds of

love and happiness;

Rising to heaven's peak as we flourish inter-passionately.

What reality brings is my heavenly queen freshly extracted

from my dreams.

My soul cannot be weathered by nature's harsh conditions.

For she shields me with her love and compassion as we sit

away in our cozy affair.

This is the season of love.

Experience Untitled

Into the wilderness of confusion, she casts out her heart to

me.

It grasps my fascination, yet I lag in the distance.

She has cut me a path through my own burdens,

Compromising the foundation that holds her peace.

As in the ultimate price of salvation, she gives up her spirit to

rejuvenate mine.

Surrendering to the needs of my affection,

She falls into my barren emotions and springs new life in me.

Her good will becomes of me with the anticipation that

likewise will she.

We evolve in a love, sweet as the nectar of a delicate rose.

Every word that rolls from our lips releases the aroma of our

passionate situation.

We glide into the mellow stream or our emotions,

The Secret Diaries of Jean Batiste

Riding the currents of a simple thought—

That we may share this experience for an eternity.

A Taste of Happiness

A taste of happiness is a delicacy to tingle the tongue

Yet when it comes, some refrain from the chance to indulge.

Even if served in open arms, one may cast away the feeling.

To refute such a treasure seems almost of mental incapacity

Or a fear to the addiction from pleasure; but no strings are

placed on happiness.

It floats freely amidst the wings of personal enjoyment

Both on the giving and receiving end.

If mere thoughts could produce such a rush, why not

participate in the full experience?

Allowing happiness to break through, receiving a taste of its

glory,

Partaking of such a heavenly emotion

Will surely bring you to your knees, exhausted in joy.

Happiness exists as on of the few rewards in life.

Life is short; happiness is scarce.

One must strive to capitalize at any given moment.

Closed minds may never feel the true passion; one must open

up.

Her Spell

Enchantress is she who holds my heart;

Beauty-stricken to the fullest extent.

Oh how I wish to merge with her

Nestled in a world, which is our own.

"You just don't know what you do to me!"

Lil' Chocolate

Rich, dark, smooth, thick,

Sweet, sensual chocolate delight

Fill my belly with your sexual calories

And satisfy my appetite.

My bed will be the fine china

On which I place my ordoive

I consume you—body, soul, and mind,

Giving you the pleasure you deserve.

You melt in my mouth

And move your body through my hands.

You taste of rare exotic fruit

Found amidst the deserted lands.

Pure, delicate, silky chocolate

You push the adrenalin through my glands,

Which pumps the infatuation of you being

As my love expands.

The Secret Diaries of Jean Batiste

I want to binge upon your flesh

As your beauty my mind ingests.

Darling chocolate you have acquired my tastes.

You satisfy me in the most intimate ways.

The G.A.M.E.*

Being a man about things—I feel—keeps me from being

caught up

Even though it burns me to the extent that I am often broken

down to the innocent young boy

In search for the loving figure to bring a remedy to my heart

ache it causes.

Pride has hardened my to heart

To ricochet any tender words I desire to speak back to my

mind.

The Secret Diaries of Jean Batiste

The backfire strikes me as a sign that things will never be

sensually sewn

For our hearts to adjoin.

But I vow to swallow such mentality for a chance to taste the

sweet nectar of your conversation.

I surrender my masculinity to gently caress the bounds of

your femininity.

That we both appear not as opposing souls, but one mind

In the moment of sacred affection; no longer masking

thoughts,

But exposing the pure feelings we have for each other.

G.A.M.E. over.

*Grown ass man excuse

The Secret Diaries of Jean Batiste

White Flag

Beyond all sexual sacraments, I offer you love, pure and true.

I surrender my destiny, my masculine indignities so that you

and I will forever be one.

Give me just a minute of you time and I'll give you mind,

body, and soul

And take the three of you I have to hold—

One moment; in hopes that it lasts a lifetime.

I've been holding back how hard I try to be reflected in your

eye at any given time,

That you see a symbol to spark memories of me.

Patience only drives my heart to fight for you love,

But anxiety sets a emotional mines on my soul,

Waiting to burst with the feelings that I have accumulated

within me.

Now I stand on the frontline, eyes fully fixed across the field

of my dreams,

The Secret Diaries of Jean Batiste

My chest pounding to the love songs playing in my ear.

I commence to move in the direction of your being and

declare my affections

With a shower of kisses to your face.

But the battle can only be won if you surrender also—

Seeming to be giving up, yet really giving in, giving us—you

and I,

Surrendering to a higher power.

A power that has conquered timelessly the bodies vulnerable

to subtle emotions.

A power making us to be forced together in chains of

commitment and admiration.

The power of love; to which I raise my white flag.

The Secret Diaries of Jean Batiste

Ms. Lady

You run through my dreams like the silkiest vanilla streams.

Pure, you are—

But causes my heart to sin.

I aim at containing you so that you cannot escape my

thought.

As you take form of my every cognition, mental clips remind

me of your fairness

Which is crowned with a beauty ages bloomed from

Aphrodite's ovaries—

Through time—

That even death play's slave to you;

Compromising the extinction of the sweet roses,

To lace each step of your stride with a delicate touch of their

fallen petals.

When others stray, you stay close to me,

Holding and squeezing the pain away,

The Secret Diaries of Jean Batiste

Comforting my thoughts as we stroll through serenity's

garden.

You give me new confidence in affection,

Showing me that through it all, I have one treasure on which

to cherish in this world.

And if it is meant to be you and me, I obligingly comply with

fate's request.

Passion was procured as optical chains linked our sight

And distance filled with blissful stares.

We now live as Siamese souls, joined at the light of first

encounter.

We flirt through space with scintillating eyes

As rustling leaves of infinite travel across autumn's bosoms.

Waltzing with fluttering hearts, we dance to the rhythm of

love,

The Secret Diaries of Jean Batiste

Imitating the sprites and nymphs whom encompasses this

enchanting feeling we have,

Urging a continuance.

Our love journeys on at a cruise control tempo,

Slowly,

Drifting into a fantasy with our eyes wide open;

Floating on a vessel of reciprocity, which produces our

buoyancy,

As you give me you and I give you me.

On one accord with reality, I remain in a trance,

Dreaming awake as I take route of life's journey on cloud

nine,

Feeling your form strum across my heart's strings like the

hum of the violin,

Singing the sound of that sweet name…Damn!

The Secret Diaries of Jean Batiste

The Secret Diaries of Jean Batiste

Knowledge

Some may not see me as the smartest man,

But there are some things I was born to understand.

And just as sure as I grow,

There are some things about this woman that I know.

I know that she is not average,

Because what beauty God plants, can no mortal man have it.

I know that she's always on my mind,

Because of the indentations on my brain her high heals have

left behind.

She is the sweetest thing I ever known,

Because she have cavities spreading from my teeth through

all of my bones.

I know she lived amidst the land of milk and honey,

Because the simple connotation leaves my mouth watering.

I know that she's an angel in disguise,

Because her halo's glow shows through my closed eyes.

The Secret Diaries of Jean Batiste

I know that I want this woman in my life,

I know that she can one day be my wife.

And if she was mine, I know what this love might be.

But what I don't know is if she wants me.

The Secret Diaries of Jean Batiste

Te necesito (En Espanol)

Necesito a alguien sostener cuando las noches crecen frías.

La lana cubre mi piel pero no mi alma.

Necesito ese beso hacer que mi corazón salta golpes.

Porque ahora su justo otra canción triste del amor que juega

en mi frecuencia.

Le necesito como mi parte del discurso.

Porque los pronombres no son profundos sin nosotros o

nosotros.

Me necesito sus ojos para mirar y ningunos otros.

Para ver su amor como reflexión del uno mismo.

Necesito amor y lo veo en usted.

Como precipitación del afecto que forma como el rocío de la

mañana.

Estoy alcanzando hacia fuera a su corazón para que comparta

conmígo.

Para dar a el míos una esperanza de la caridad.

The Secret Diaries of Jean Batiste

Y puesto que era una víctima de la soledad así que usted marchó de largo adentro como Ejército de Salvamento y me rescató con sus brazos anchos se abre y un corazón caliente. Tan en vuelta le doy que todo I posee, pues tomo a su mano cada medida de modo que usted sea allí conmígo un curso de la vida, compensándole para su caridad.

The Secret Diaries of Jean Batiste

I Need You (In English)

I need someone to hold when the nights grow cold.

The wool blankets my skin but not my soul.

I need that kiss to make my heart skip beats.

Because now its just another sad love song playing on my

frequency.

I need you as my part of speech.

Because pronouns are not profound without us or we.

I need your eyes in which to look—and no one else's.

To see your love as a reflection of self.

I need love and I see it in you.

As a precipitation of affection forming like the morning dew.

I am reaching out to your heart for it to share with me.

To give mine a hope for charity.

And since I was a victim of loneliness so long

You marched in as Salvation Army and rescued me with your

arms wide open and a warm heart.

The Secret Diaries of Jean Batiste

So in return I give you everything I own,

As I take your hand each step so that you are there with me a

lifetime, repaying you for your charity.

50

The Secret Diaries of Jean Batiste

Beloved

Her presence has a hand in existence—

Being the mother of the greatest gifts of nature.

As she walks, she plants seeds of vegetation,

Leaving the fruit of her labor behind, painting a luscious

landscape.

Her smile feeds photosynthetic reactions,

Illuminating the emerald fields with rich leaves and stems.

Hazel-auburn speckled jewels shine in her eyes,

Holding true the hidden treasures of the earth.

Her voice whispers sweet nothings in nature's ear that excites

life into flourishment.

Her breath could create life in a solemn stone—

So pure that inhaling it stimulates even taste buds like

crystalline sugar.

Her touch is the only sense—next the Heavens—that is

gentle enough to hold the clouds in form.

With one wave of her hand, she sculpts intimate scenery into

the skies,

Accenting its innocent baby-blue background.

Her being is a necessity to bring the natural and wondrous

fruit out of her surroundings

For she epitomizes Beauty!

Dream Lover

Fairytale to biography is my transfiguring genre;

Taking this love story from abstract to concrete.

Eyes wide shut, I sleep in open consciousness of what I am

witnessing—

I see silhouettes sway in-synch with her lip-song, searing my

eardrums,

Leaving passion marks on my mind.

Her hips swung between me and dreaming to seemingly

reality—

Burst shatterings gleaming—glittering in the power of my

bottled genie.

Then with three strokes, the awakened entity waves her wand

across my thinking;

Granting access to my premonitions.

The Secret Diaries of Jean Batiste

More than three wishes could bring, she sprinkles love like
the essence of spring,

And now I am sprung.

Her magic makes resistance numb as she strums my
endorphins till I function in a slumber;

Prying my emotions wide open to expose vulnerability, she
steals my heart

With the might of forty thieves in lure of my captivity,

Trapping me in servitude, waiting to be wished free.

But through similar mediums as she has enslaved me, I am
also her master—

So the mystery would be—as I unleash my own feat of magic.

These exchanged tactics chains our souls in placid cohesion.

It is clear that to a high degree fondness holds me, controls
me, and grows for me

As it shows in her acquisition of my being.

The Secret Diaries of Jean Batiste

For of all the mortal souls suspended in matter, she found

mine to feed her fancy.

And this mystic attraction mimics fairy fantasy.

Like anything I have ever lived, it did not seem to be.

So indeed did I live…a dream…a…dream.

Utopia

Deep in the sea of seclusion, sunset seals our infusion

As you sink into my arms and watch the heavens lie down to

bed.

The moon rises and casts a halo around your head—eclipsed

by the presence of your beauty—

Crowning you the queen our surroundings,

And begging entrance into our intimate dimension.

We levitate to our feet and join in-step with the dancing stars.

The tempo slows as our mental flow thickens like the mussels

ornamenting the island sheets.

Nothing between us has air to breathe.

So close that we can exist as one being, we glide across the

sandy shores to silent love songs,

Playing to the rhythm of our racing hearts—rapping more

with each glimpse of one another.

In such instances, we find weakness invading

The Secret Diaries of Jean Batiste

As our collapsing limbs lead us on path with the horizon.

The next moment, not even the crashing waves can penetrate

our soundproof interests.

Wrapped in what heat we generate, the temperature makes

our condition less and less to bare.

Southern breezes are all that blanket our bodies, which lay in

original texture blended with crystal grains.

There we remain till ocean currents stain our contour on the

coastal floor,

That when we arise, our memory will be imprinted as a

signature to what we have...

Amazing Love

My world spins with you as my axis,

The center of my emotions, and my pivotal satisfaction;

And the fact is that practice cannot perfect this feeling

As I fumble my phrases—

Caught in a maze; lost and dazed from this amazing love.

Raised above the tests and trials have our time been placed in

Karma's palm

To secure our capture in this rapturous feeling—flying high

in each other's affection.

A reflection of you afflicted my memory and stained my mind

with each moment

From first encounter to current interaction.

My attraction, then and now—

The wait—

Separate paths,

The Secret Diaries of Jean Batiste

And fate shows our place here to be meant.

Our early meetings were marked with innocence and signs of

bliss.

Growing so personal, we touched but never kissed;

Aimed at love's trajectory but arrows missed;

So split apart—but still in my heart is the thought of having

you in my life.

And through the years I have wished to be sent a guardian of

the heavens,

And so she went—but I have returned;

Here to earn what was almost lost;

Yearning to collect at any cost the chance to once more be at

your heal—

To once more feel perfect submission to you;

With this chance being a true attempt at what started out

as...

So amazing!

Eternal Chain

Eternal chain of love acquire its links—

My soul,

My heart,

My hands,

My lips;

Clasps them to their counterparts—

Her soul,

Her heart,

Her hands,

Her lips;

Our eternal chain of love is composed—

One soul,

One heart,

Hand-in-hand,

Tender kisses.

Are You There?

We bonded on sudden terms, but fusion firmed each time I

heard your voice

Of sweet melody and harmonic chords.

As a lonely star at it's death, falls to unleash wishful thinking,

So have I fallen for you;

Wishing to combine into one mind, entering a love groove.

But are you real?

Do you want to soar high in Cupid's eye?

Or am I being taken on a ride to come, not to a dead end, but

to a friend?

If you take my heart and hold it, don't let it go.

Or torture it painfully and slowly through the punishment of

rejection.

The Secret Diaries of Jean Batiste

Feel my affection if you are real—fluent and true;

All the love that I have for you;

To be received only by open arms.

Don't be afraid , there's no harm in love.

Our own love zone is what we will make,

To ecstasy is where I'll take you,

Discovering the deepest thoughts and most tender spots of

each other's

heavenly temples.

To reach the depth of your love is my quest;

Finding the river of satisfaction that breaks the dam

At the highest point of heated passion.

It was eternal bliss when we first crossed souls

Our lips caught a hold, with the touch of rose petals.

The Secret Diaries of Jean Batiste

It was heaven from there, like I had never felt before.

Will it ever end or did it ever begin?

I open my eyes and see what stands before me—the answer

to my proposal,

Which has been dangling from your lips, but soon slipped,

Toying with my anxiety.

Are you there?

The Secret Diaries of Jean Batiste

The Song of the Wind

Have you ever heard the song of the wind,

As gentle as the stroke of a rose petal breezing across the

skin?

It's all that soothes my aching heart,

Slammed shut with denial by one who I tried to let in.

The sweet sound comes and touches my soul

In the spots where pain has done its deed.

The rustling notes surround me, wrapping me in its melody,

Stopping the escape of gentle thoughts that I bleed.

This song keeps me going along with God's grace and

strength—

It's all I need to get by.

I hope my prayers are blown to heaven, entangled in a wind

song;

And may God send me an angel from the sky.

The wind song blows through loneliness, which is heard

frequently in my ears—

And can only be plugged by love.

Love that is special to my mind, body , and soul;

That I send a praise of thanksgiving through a wind song,

above.

The Secret Diaries of Jean Batiste

cK-one

Wondering in a field of loneliness,

I discover a gentle flower,

Whose beauty stunned my heart,

Stopping its beat with such an entrancing power.

Flirtatious features work their magic

As I discover her wondrous being,

Stripping me of all vocal vowels

As I gaze upon the treasure, in which I am seeing.

As do precious jewels, her eyes sparkle,

Combining with the light of her smile,

Shining a ray of love in my heart,

Greater than a love for mother by child.

Her skin, with its natural touch

The Secret Diaries of Jean Batiste

Is silky as petals against my skin

Appealing to all of my senses

My caresses may never end.

Her voice is as soft as a passing breeze,

Her words, soft-spoken like the clouds.

Incapable of withstanding her dazzling qualities,

It makes my heart beat loud.

I pick my flower up, inhaling her aroma

Rich as the fragrance of vanilla fields.

She holds my very thoughts and acts,

That to every command I yield.

I hold her against my chest,

Her presence accentuates the room.

Her body pressed firmly to mine,

She is my heavenly perfume.

The Secret Diaries of Jean Batiste

Inside (Feeling You – part II)

To see you is to be you—your body cavity through

Your bodily metabolic, systolic, and diastolic pressures.

No one can measure the whole nine I'm going just to feel

your senses;

Your taste and touch intensifies at your melting point

To the direction of your feminine vectors;

Acute appendages becoming obtuse;

Open to suggestive advances, temple erections invade your

foundation—so shaky, Trembles and vapors penetrating in

your mind's elations.

Your expectations already have been exceeded—ecstasy, the

"why?" deleted.

Delighted and invited to your private party.

You the V.I.P. and me the guest of honor.

Inside intimate dwellings, entangled and interstellar

The dreams and fantasies combined to one majestic moment.

The Secret Diaries of Jean Batiste

More components make up the total—flesh and bone

mimicking mortal

Composition from the position, intermission being omitted.

Committed to only you, confined bodily through your mind,

Down your spine and other extremities.

Inside your body, soul, and mind I know that you are feeling

me.

The Secret Diaries of Jean Batiste

The Greatest Conversation

Picture-perfect phases painted are stained in my memory

Of me cradling her cognitions to get acquainted.

I maintained it for a minute.

Whether you send it or receive it,

Communications go beyond the sheets of spoken words.

It is the action verbs acting out intensions.

The truth, full throttle is too hard to swallow;

So I spit out first impressions.

No interjections or conjunctions, simply conjoined at the lips;

Soft-spoken syllables signing on the dotted line of our verbal

contract,

From eye contact to finger-tips.

I slipped past the wrist-line, making my way through body,

soul and mind;

The Secret Diaries of Jean Batiste

Ignoring velocity.

Top down, you can find me rolling through mental traffic,

obeying all signals;

The point of destination pivotal.

The turning point of access—absessed organs from over

exertion of my heart.

Could it be love at first sight?

Or did I bite more than I could chew,

Spewing out my feelings in a repetitive statement

To make this engagement spin out of control, but take off

weightless.

No time wasted; straight to the point, but paced;

To get the full taste of this...the greatest conversation.

The Secret Diaries of Jean Batiste

On the D.L.

I do agree that she's out of my league,

But the feelings she feeds are more than fanatic.

Being just a fool to believe that I fill even a twitch's glance in

her eye

Cheers me on to enquire of my chance,

But I withdraw.

Though my imagination has taken her heart for ransom,

Reality has reversed roles,

As my captivation by her timelessly preserved beauty

Has left my soul searching for salvation.

But what intrigues me the most is that she doesn't even

notice me.

Even though my emotions seep through the holes of hope

and desperation—

The Secret Diaries of Jean Batiste

Me having thoughts that open arms guide her body to the

source of my expectations.

Yet such determination shows my profession of infatuation

Contested with the nature of our actual relationship—

Being congested of extraordinary circumstance;

All too eccentric to circumvent common law.

So do I draw the line?

Though it is not love-hate, sentimental boundaries hold me

not to tarry on her territory.

So the love I create remains on mental grounds.

And no to trespass on the moment, I hold it inside the walls

of rationality.

To think we were on the same page was a fallacy.

Her personality shows her to be well educated in the laws of

affection,

But I'm just an undergraduate.

The Secret Diaries of Jean Batiste

Supernatural Woman

Shed the modesty, I bet your name is goddess

Because mythological majesty transcribes your biography

And reality airs an essence of immortality with an everlasting

beauty

Possessing the strength to pin my heart against a love-struck

epiphany.

Rich ethnicity immerges through your body language,

Abstained from correspondence with word in absentia.

Not to mention that my passes are being deflected.

As a neglected child, I wonder the empty emotions with the

latchkey around my neck.

Unmatched to the deadbolt, I beg entrance but remain

porched in my affection,

Imploring that you remove the restraints.

The Secret Diaries of Jean Batiste

But quaint traditions call for a formal introduction before
attaining access.

Shall I address you in this lifetime or wait until the next?
When we breath the dust from the butterfly's wings and
canaries sing in a native tongue
As we wade amidst a million twinkling stars, orbiting the
center of the universe—
Your beautiful being that also rules my world.

And words cannot fill this space in such an instant mark of
time and place
That I call my life,
So I embrace you to absorb your energy because it is eternal,
according to physical laws.

What we have can neither be created nor destroyed,

The Secret Diaries of Jean Batiste

Only transformed into the present state of the matter;

The fact that I have fallen for an unearthly entity;

For you are truly supernatural.

The Secret Diaries of Jean Batiste

A Letter of Love's Odyssey

Dear Love,

It been so long since I've been away that you can

count the hours with the months—24;

Which adds another day onto the heartbreak.

Yet however long it takes I'm coming to be with you, so have

patience and let me have my say.

I'm sorry, baby, but I'll be home late; warm my plate and chill

the wine.

I'm still on time because the gate is still open with no line in

waiting.

I'm negating the weather. Whether it's cold, crisp, clear, or

raining, I'm still remaining

Focused on my destination; the final reservation being set for

me to be on my way.

The Secret Diaries of Jean Batiste

Though midnight chimes, I'm still on time; I'm just in the

wrong place;

High above the ground instead of below your waist.

I know the tears pour on your face and it's hard to breathe

but believe me when I promise —

I'll be there.

I know you wonder how I can say that when I'll be late,

But baby still warm my plate and chill the wine.

My tardiness is irrelevant because my clock ticks by quality

time;

The hands in perfect position, expressing my punctuality.

Although our love is past due, I will make it up to you as

soon as I can.

When I get there, I'll take your hand gently and awake you

from your sleep;

The Secret Diaries of Jean Batiste

Slip your feet from the covers and spread you across the silk

sheets;

The rest I'll leave to your imagination—think about it as you

await my arrival.

But for now, I'll be home late so warm my plate and chill the

wine.

I'm coming home tonight.

The Secret Diaries of Jean Batiste

How I Felt on 02-06-04

(On the Surface)

It's like stepping into mud holes or standing by the road in

the rain

And getting soaked by an unconcerned driver—

In the cold, shivering to the bone on your long walk—

umbrella blown inside out—

Having a deep desire to return home but perseverance pushes

you forward until you get there—

Body saturated—all but your hair—making rhythms with the

squishing sound of your socks like water spouts—

You get inside with nowhere to dry, and slide from your own

collected precipitation—

Waiting for the day to roll by, but the time seems to run like

molasses in January—

The Secret Diaries of Jean Batiste

But you remain in the greatest delight because despite the

travel out, the return home to someone special is so

magical—

That's how you make me feel.

You shield my heart from the harsh weather and internalize

more pleasant conditions...

The Secret Diaries of Jean Batiste

How I Felt on 02-06-04

(Deep Within)

I petition my flesh in yours as feelings pour through thoughts

of your thickness

More than water for chocolate kisses upon your lips,

But I don't bother to stop the wishes that reality missed.

My spoken words rap upon your eardrum,

Penetrating your brain and pressing your lungs because I hear

heavy breathing;

Leading me on the path of destructive diction,

Breaking down the will to resist as I mention methods to feed

my desire;

You put my soul through the fire that burns bright in the

light of your illuminating eyes complemented by your smile.

You take me miles away from ordinary and that's why you are

on my mind;

Making it so that I can't wait to return home.

Amber Rose

No one knows how my heart grows,

Swelling from the pressure of your essence on my senses

As I commence to explore the shores of your mind to the

depth of your soul.

Never knowing such treasure existed, I behold

Your smile stretching to imagination's coast with sunset at its

end,

Composing an amber rose that glows through my every

thought;

Going to show the way to your heart.

There lies the source of what holds you to be such a caring

and giving being.

Seeing such light brightens even the darkest valleys and erases

fear.

The Secret Diaries of Jean Batiste

A light flowered by the hands of one so incredible

That she endlessly brightens the skies.

She epitomizes all that is heavenly.

Symbolized by none other than…an amber rose.

The Secret Diaries of Jean Batiste

Fallen

I saw a wounded angel struggling across heaven's

view; broken-hearted in a delicate mold.

Though a mortal man like me cannot touch her, I can send

wishes of serenity through silent prayers.

Bowed down, I close my eyes as to converse with the entity,

expressing my comfort in a soothing melody—

"Heavenly being,

take wings and return home;

down-trodden is not a feeling in which to dwell upon.

You serve much more purpose in this realm—

bringing a passionate joy just from your presence.

But being one made so sweet from the nectar dripping from

God's goblet,

it puzzles me why you cry.

Pretty brown eyes are lackluster when filled with

saturation.

The Secret Diaries of Jean Batiste

Send those tears to the sky that they give youth

delight.

Sorrow should sew no seeds in your heart because

you are beautiful.

Return home and sit once again upon your pedestal.

You are much too precious to be lost in the depths of

sadness.

For the energy it takes to find another as amazing as

you would place a wrinkle in time and space."

The Secret Diaries of Jean Batiste

The Rebirth

What makes me special is the spontaneous passion beyond

the threshold;

Presently inside your vessel;

Flesh is so weak and tender from point that I enter to the

ripples;

Pulse as rapid as it is in your temple;

Mentally metastasized;

Filling your eyes to tears rolling down your thighs;

Moisturized in my love, inside;

Guided by muscular contractions,

Forcing the reaction of welts down my spine;

From you gripping my back during the ride;

With motion simultaneous and animated as we come alive.

The Secret Diaries of Jean Batiste

A Toast to Love

This one is dedicated to...

The one I can't live without even if she's not with me;

The one that I constantly seek and find for her to blindly lead me;

The one for whom I would do anything and ask for nothing in return;

The one for which my heart yearns; who ignites my desires; also, from whom I've been burned;

The one who is more potent than money or power;

The one that not only possesses the ball and chain, but the master key, the lock, the armed guards, and the watchtower;

The one we all want, we need, we fear, and we hope to experience at least once;

The one that in good times puts me on cloud nine, but in bad can put me six feet under.

The Secret Diaries of Jean Batiste

The one I live for, fight for, and die;

The one to whom I give my all, for her to constantly take and

take until my well runs dry;

The one that should not cost a thing, but to whom I've lost

my sense from her driving me insane;

To love...

Such a beautiful thing that I will have another shot.

Conclusion

What you have just witnessed was a look inside the mind of a man who clearly expresses an obsession for the opposite sex. Some of his works were so delicate that for personal reasons, the names originally found at the end of each poem were taken out. However, there is no denying that the subjects to whom the dedications were given would have no problem deciphering her acknowledgment. Indeed the reason for such is to keep from revealing his most intimate secrets. Yet, the poems do put his heart on display with the detail of each line written. This has been a discovery inside the *Secret Diaries of Jean Batiste.*

The Secret Diaries of Jean Batiste

About the Author

Nigel Walker was born February 13, 1980 to Jacqueline and David Walker. He was born and raised in Eufaula, AL by his mother along with seven brothers and sisters.

He has been writing poetry since he was about 11 years old and continues today to paint vivid pictures through the expressions of poetry. His works have been published in several literary magazines, such as *Early Spring*, the *Menagerie*, and the *Scroll*. He has also received acclaim in various poetry contests such as Poetry.com. He has made several public performances, including a guest performance for Stess the Emcee, who opened for Cee-lo in concert on the campus of LaGrange College; and serving a regular at LaGrange College's Spoken Word session called the *Cypher*. He also appeared in an Independent Artist showcase at the former Club Shine in Atlanta, GA.

The Secret Diaries of Jean Batiste

Though his first love is being a teacher, which he
pursues full-time, he continues to entertain the mind and soul
with his lyrical expressions.

The Secret Diaries of Jean Batiste

About the Book

The Secret Diaries of Jean Batiste is a fictionalized representation of the author's real-life endeavors and trials of romance, and his undying infatuation of women. The character Jean Batiste was originally created to show someone struggling through the identity of his ancestry as seen in the first introductory poem, but was developed into one of a romantic poet, using his French name as a hook. Though they do not share the same background, the fictional character is a close representation of the author.

Each poem in the work is personalized by true feelings held for the subject to which it was dedicated. The dedications are truly heart-felt during the times that they were made; which explains the importance of including each one in the work. The names originally placed at the end of each poem were taken out because the author felt that releasing actual names would create a personal conflict among in his personal acquaintances. The final presentation of his work was done in order to avoid controversy in order to share his art of lyrical expression.

www.ingramcontent.com/pod-product-compliance
Lightning Source LLC
LaVergne TN
LVHW011214080426
835508LV00007B/784